But It's My Day

A Wedding Handbook for Bridezillas

TEAL MITCHELL

ISBN: 1468010220
ISBN-13: 9781468010220

Who This Book Is For

This book is for brides-to-be, bridesmaids, and anyone who is in any danger of coming into close proximity of a bride(zilla). This book is meant to entertain you and serve as a useful guide to help you laugh your way through till the day of the wedding. Please accept this small token of "tough love" from me to you.

—Teal Mitchell

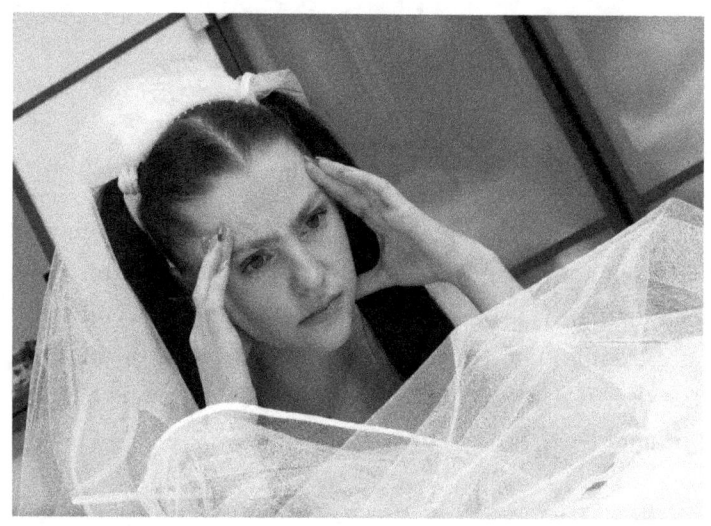

Why You Need This Book

This book is not your typical wedding etiquette book. It serves as a sort of how-to guide based on my experiences working the wedding circuit as a stylist for the past thirteen years. If you want to avoid the unnecessary mistakes that most bridezillas—I mean, women—make once they've gotten caught up in the whirlwind of wedding planning, then you will read this book before you begin the process, and will refer back to it as often as needed.

Dedication

This book is dedicated to everyone (past and present) at Tivon Salon and Spa.

Introduction

Since you are reading this book, I'm assuming that there is one question *YOU* are asking yourself right now: Am I really a bridezilla?

You're telling yourself: No. Not me. Couldn't be. But the truth is, more than likely, you are. Most bridezillas are unaware that they belong to this club of insanity.

Hey, put it this way: If someone tells you that you're being a bridezilla, you should believe it. As a matter of fact, if someone even uses this term in your presence, he or she has probably pegged you as a bridezilla waiting to happen. Some of the people around you are either too nice or too scared to let you know that your behavior is a bit bridezilla-ish, so what they'll do is drop subtle hints of other bridezilla situations that they know about, hoping you'll get the picture.

But, you don't get it, because you've already entered— "The Bridezilla Zone"! (Music: Duh-nuh-nuh-nuh, duh-nuh-nuh-nuh…remember? *The Twilight Zone*? Never mind.)

Well, don't worry; you can still be saved from the abyss.

Keep reading, and enjoy!

Bridezilla Defined

Origin: 1990s

Blend of Bride and Godzilla (Japanese movie monster)

Bridezilla ~ A woman whose behavior in planning her wedding is regarded as obsessive or intolerably demanding.

—Oxford Dictionary

Bridezilla ~ A new breed of soon-to-be-wed women who abuse the idea that weddings are their "day." They terrorize their bridal party and family members, make greedy demands, and break all rules of etiquette to ensure that they are the single most important person on the planet from the time they are engaged to the time they are married.

—Urban Dictionary

Oooh! Harsh.

Bridezillas in Action

A bridezilla will:

- Set herself up with grueling schedules
- Become unreasonable about losing weight
- Have no problem blowing her wedding budget, even if it means being homeless afterward. At least she can say that she had a beautiful wedding, right?

Vendors

This is what your vendors list probably looks like:

- Wedding Planner
- Florist
- Hairstylist
- Makeup Artist
- Deejay
- Band
- Caterer
- Photographer
- Venue Operator
- Etc., etc.

It would be in your best interest to try and keep from offending these people. These are the people who assist you in making your Special Day so memorable. So, verbally attacking these folks won't be a good idea. You want them to actually show up and do their job, don't you?

Note: Feed Your Vendors! Remember, they have been working tirelessly to make "it" all happen for you. Feed them well and they are sure to keep their energy up and going strong, just to get you through the Big Day! Plus, it will distract them from focusing on your bridezilla ways. And it will give them at least one nice thing to say about you when the gossip fest about *YOU* and your wedding begins.

Believe it or not, your vendors have other clients besides you. I know you would like to think that your wedding is the only thing that matters to them, and that they are working around the clock, just for *YOU*.

But, the truth of the matter is: This is their job. This is how they earn a living!

So, of course they are working with other clients. And this is OK, and perfectly acceptable. You will find that professionals tend to utilize schedules in order to work with multiple people. Therefore, it's very important for you to be as respectful of their time as you can.

Please, no after-hours phone calls! That's just tacky.

Pay Up!

———————

Set aside some time a few days before the wedding to go over who you owe $$$ to. Write those checks ahead of time, while you still have the opportunity to do so before all the chaos begins.

Trust me; it is extremely easy to forget to pay your service providers when you have a million things on your mind. These people do expect to be paid promptly. So, don't accidentally stiff them. They will harass you until they are paid.

No bad checks allowed. Thanks.

Opinions, Opinions, Everybody Has Them

———— ▬ ————

You definitely want to be open to accepting expert opinions.

Remember: You hired these people, so let them do their job. You'll be glad you did. And don't worry; you won't be handing over too much creative control.

You + Expert/Professional = Partnership

With that said, one of the quickest ways to spark a bridezilla situation is for the bride to accept too many outside opinions from friends and family. These people love you and just want to help.

But beware: This can and will stress you out. So, minimize the outside input. Trust your own instincts and the professionals.

Gifts

Please try to be thoughtful in this area. Remember that your bridesmaids, parents, and future in-laws have been putting up with you since the first day this whole wedding business began.

So, when choosing a gift, keep in mind that you don't have to buy anything super expensive and extravagant—although you should exercise your creativity.

Purchasing your people a cheesy pair of fake pearl earrings that you expect them to wear only for your wedding is not acceptable.

They will think you are a thoughtless jerk for giving a gift like that. Surely, you can be a little more creative in showing the people you love and care about how much you appreciate them?

Hey, they must love you, too; they did sign up for all this.

Bridesmaids

Guess what? Your bridesmaids can't afford the dress you picked out for them.

They are already going to be behind on next month's rent due to the other costs associated with your wedding.

- Traveling expenses
- Wedding gifts
- Bachelorette party
- And other hidden costs

So, spare them the pain of high-priced dresses they may never get to wear again. And, please don't choose ugly dresses on purpose. That's just weird.

Oh! And another thing: Don't have your heart set on your bridesmaids wearing the exact same dress. (Unless of course you plan to replace your bridesmaids with clones for this special occasion.)

Take into consideration what looks best for each individual. What looks good on one person may not look so good on someone else. Trying to make everyone look alike can turn a beautiful dress into an ugly one very quickly.

The same goes for hair. It's impossible to have everyone wear the exact same hairstyle, OK? Hey! You could order them all the same wig. Afro wigs for everybody! Yay!

Let's Party!

Having your bachelorette party the night before the wedding is a BIG no-no! Why would you do this? Way too many things can go wrong:

- You'll be sick
- You'll look like crap
- You're already a bridezilla and this will just make it worse

So, keep it very low-key the night before. Choose sleeping over "kicking it" half the night.

Also, be sure not to make any assumptions that someone from your wedding party will be the DD (designated driver) for the night of your bachelorette party.

This isn't actually required of your staff. Oops! Excuse me. I mean your bridesmaids. They want to kick back and have fun just as much as you do. So please, make the proper arrangements ahead of time for how you want this to go down so that there are no mishaps.

You should consider using some sort of car service (cab, limo, helicopter, whatever). The main goal is that everyone get to and from the destination safely.

Who's Paying for This?

Let's face it: Times have changed. The rules have changed. The bride's family no longer has to be responsible for the biggest portion of wedding costs. Neither does the groom's family.

Here's a concept: This is YOUR wedding. Why don't you and your groom-to-be put your two heads together and figure out how you can pay for this on your own?

Now, just wait a minute, Bridezilla. Hear me out on this before you get angry and snap your girdle.

There are a couple of practical reasons behind my theory:

1.) The less money you put in, the less creative control you have. The person holding the cash has the power. And your wedding quickly becomes the vision of someone else. Period.

2.) Tell me something: Do you plan on helping Mom and Dad replenish their savings or add to their retirement accounts after they've footed the bill for your wedding that cost thousands of dollars? Eh? Didn't think so.

TEAL MITCHELL

Details, Details, Details

Guess what else? No one cares about how many napkins you ordered, or that your custom-made veil recently came in from Paris or wherever.

So, just chill out on these types of discussions. The only people who could possibly be interested in these sorts of details are parents and bridesmaids. And they can only take conversations like this in very small doses.

I know this is tough to hear, but I'm going to say it anyway: Your wedding is not the first thing on other people's minds.

They do have lives that they are living, ya know? They already have your wedding recorded on their calendars and in their planners. Remember? You sent out save-the-date cards.

So, trust that everyone will show up. Hopefully.

Boo! Aaaahhhh!

Hey, all the nightmares you've been having about your dress falling apart or not fitting you...

Are not real!

So, knowing this, you can relax. Lots of brides have these types of nightmares. Just ignore them.

Besides, you have scheduled fittings to look forward to. Your dress will be fine.

Uninvited Guests

———— ————

As for the Wedding Crashers: Pay them no mind, because there's not much you can do about them anyway—unless of course you would like to cause a scene at your wedding.

Is it a tacky move to show up at someone's wedding uninvited?

Sure it is. But you're in wedding bliss at the point this is occurring. So, let someone else deal with this matter, or simply let it go.

Here Comes the Groom

Hey, Bridezilla! Did you forget that you're not going to be marrying yourself on the day of your wedding? This is your fiancé's wedding also.

It would be really nice if you would take into consideration some of the thoughts and ideas of your groom-to-be. You do want this to be an event that is memorable and enjoyable for you both, right?

Trust that your guy knows and understands that you've been fantasizing about your wedding since you were eight years old, and he doesn't want to step on your toes.

In the midst of all your vigorous planning, just remember that he still exists.

You could at least let him request that those stupid songs (which you hate) be played at the reception. I'm just saying…

Deep breaths, one…two…three…

Choose Sanity

―――

Not giving yourself enough time to plan your wedding is a sure way to inflict pain upon yourself and others. A sane bride-to-be will give herself at least a year or more to plan. I believe that is the industry standard.

So, don't get any bright ideas and decide that you're going to try to plan a huge and elaborate wedding in less than four weeks.

At this point, please consider eloping. Thanks.

What to Avoid

If you feel yourself suddenly getting the urge to participate in these types of behaviors:

- Yelling
- Kicking
- Screaming
- Throwing things
- Cursing
- Crying for what may seem to be no reason at all

DON'T.

Do you really want to look like a jackass?

Size Does Matter

———

1 bridezilla + 10 bridesmaids = Hell

Now, don't get me wrong; it's a woman's prerogative to have as many people in her wedding as she wants.

All I'm saying is: If you want to be able to control your stress level, you will not have a wedding party that is this large.

Sometimes wedding parties get this big because the bride is afraid that she'll offend someone by not asking her to participate in the festivities.

Allow me to let you in on a little secret: Half of the ten you're planning on asking don't want to be in your wedding anyway.

Reasons:

1.)   They can't afford it

2.)   They've gained weight

3.)   They were in two weddings last year, and would rather vomit for three days than be a bridesmaid again.

Oh, and Another Thing...

I feel this is worth mentioning: Do not compare yourself to magazine brides, or any other bride.

It's a total waste of time, and you should be focused on more productive things. If you want to be happy on your wedding day, you will tailor everything around what best fits your own individual style.

Elvis theme wedding, anyone?

Last Words

Don't Miss Your Wedding!

What I mean by this is: Don't get so caught up in all the things going wrong that are beyond your control, like messed-up seating charts, or even the groom's drunk uncle nodding off over in the corner.

So many brides have said that their wedding was a complete blur to them, because they were sidetracked by things which they later discovered really didn't matter at all.

Don't let this happen to *YOU*!

You've already made sure that the handling of all the details has been delegated to someone else, right? Your only job at this point is to simply have fun.

Dos

1.) DO be clear with everyone about what you want. This means vendors, wedding party, family, and anyone involved. Simple.

2.) DO bring a picture with you when you see your stylist. Only one or two will be acceptable. Any more than that—you're probably a bridezilla.

3.) DO make itineraries! As clichéd as it sounds, they are an excellent tool. This allows everyone to know where, when, and what's going on at all times.

4.) DO budget for a full and open bar at your reception. Everyone will appreciate it.

5.)   DO schedule your phone calls/meetings with your vendors. By doing so, you are being respectful of other people's time.

6.)   DO be realistic about your budget. Try not to forget that you have to come back to the "real world" after the wedding is over.

Don'ts

1.) DON'T schedule a trial run for your hair until you have your veil or headpiece.

2.) DON'T schedule more than one or two trial-run appointments for your hair. Do you really need any more than that?

3.) DON'T call your wedding vendors every day, twice a day.

4.) DON'T plan your wedding around another event. Not smart.

5.) DON'T have anyone from your wedding party clean up after the reception. They'll be way too exhausted to take on this task. Arrange for someone outside of the wedding party to do the cleanup. Your people will love you for this one.

6.)   DO NOT, under any circumstances, let anyone hear you use the phrase, "But, it's *MY* day!" (especially in a whiny voice). That's just annoying.